**ANCHOR BOOKS**

THE CLASSIC COLLECTION OF VILLANELLE

Edited by

Kelly Deacon

First published in Great Britain in 2000 by
ANCHOR BOOKS
Remus House,
Coltsfoot Drive,
Woodston,
Peterborough, PE2 9JX
Telephone (01733) 898102

Copyright Contributors 1999

HB ISBN 1 85930 762 0
SB ISBN 1 85930 767 1

FOREWORD

There are many reasons why people turn to the written form, perhaps as a form of relief or a way to express one's feelings. A lot of the time it is a tragedy or some form of celebration that inspires a person to put pen to paper. Often people, friends and family, pets, hobbies and places, lend themselves as a subject on which to centre our poetry.

However *The Classic Collection of Villanelle* is a little different. All the poets in this collection were presented a challenge - to write a poem to the very specific style of the villanelle. Each poet has a different story to tell or message to spread - however they have risen to the challenge with vigour and excellence.

So sit back and allow this inspiring poetic form to fill your mind, become one with not only the written word but the villanelle as well.

Kelly Deacon
Editor

CONTENTS

VILLANELLE

My courage is starting to fade away:
Wouldn't you like to hear why?
Someone is bullying, thinking it's play.

I wish I didn't have to stay,
Give all my enemies a nervous 'Hi.'
My courage is starting to fade away.

My best is done to hide each day,
They call me names, I cry,
Someone is bullying, thinking it's play.

Ice underneath an angry sun's ray;
Like a bird, I yearn to fly,
My courage is starting to fade away.

Nothing done wrong, why do I pay?
Imaginary rights, please fall from the sky,
Someone is bullying, thinking it's play.

'Rights do exist,' some people say,
I'll never understand, why they do lie:
My courage is starting to fade away,
Someone is bullying, thinking it's play.

Parivash Jeelani (11)

GOING DOWN

Descending to the sunken wood
You glanced at me with tear stung face,
Blindly. You never understood.

You thought I had come back for good,
Shaken him off without a trace.
Descending to the sunken wood,

Leaving the bright heath where we'd stood,
Stumbling into that deep, dark place
Blindly, you never understood.

Far off larks sang. A shadow flood
Closed round us in a chill embrace,
Descending to the sunken wood.

You'd shaken off your sombre mood,
Seemed to be searching each tree's base
Blindly. You never understood

I loved him, turned triumphant, showed
Me white violets, fragile as lace,
Descending to the sunken wood,
Blindly. You never understood.

Andria Cooke

ONE BRIGHT RED ROSE

One bright red rose in September
Reminds me so much about you
So I will always remember

Your lips are so soft and tender
As a petal laden with dew
One bright red rose in September

Beauteous hair; colour of amber
Scent as delicate, as the hue
So I will always remember

A wish for hope in November
Truth that eternally comes through
One bright red rose in September

My love still a glowing ember
I will never ever forget you
So I will always remember

To you my heart I surrender
Think of you forever, I do
One bright red rose in September
So I will always remember.

Len Beddow

OUT OF TOUCH AND INCOMMUNICADO

Isolation kept the world locked out;
It provided a cell not a sanctuary,
I served my time inside in doubt.

Silence my solitary keep throughout;
Never broke on sounds of repartee,
Isolation kept the world locked out.

I prayed someone might let me out;
Or proclaim the next day liberty,
I served my time inside in doubt.

Walls held firm to muffle my shout;
Windows drew only my face to see,
Isolation kept the world locked out.

In that redoubt and all else without;
I questioned the muse with soliloquy,
I served my time inside in doubt.

Scarlet the fever barred my way out;
So we wrested until I broke free,
Isolation kept the world locked out,
I served my time inside in doubt.

S R Green

GOODBYE TO LOVE

Be gone; be gone from me,
That lovers lie of old,
Be gone sweet memory.

Blind my eyes so not to see,
You look at me so cold,
Be gone; be gone from me.

I do not want your company,
No thoughts will I behold,
Be gone sweet memory.

Depart the love I had for thee,
It can not be bought or sold,
Be gone; be gone from me.

I beg you hear my plea,
Please do as you're told,
Be gone sweet memory.

Taint not my future for it must be,
A story yet untold,
Be gone; be gone from me,
Be gone sweet memory.

S A Ward

A LIFETIME'S LOVE

Whenever you are feeling blue
And you question why
Remember always, I love you.

We live a life that's good and true
And this you can't deny
Whenever you are feeling blue

Built to last our whole lives through
We don't even have to try
Remember always, I love you.

Even when difficult times are due
Tears no longer cry
Whenever you are feeling blue

We are one and not two
With hearts so full of joy
Remember always, I love you.

Recall the day we said 'I do'
With a sparkle in your eye
Whenever you are feeling blue
Remember always, I love you.

Dennis N Davies

WATCHING

As I watch the people passing by
So many deep in thought
Sometimes a laugh, or just a sigh

A nod by some or no reply
A lot just seem distraught
As I watch the people passing by

A lot just live a lie
Minds intent on what they've bought
Sometimes a laugh, or just a sigh

Other times a look may catch my eye
Or a sound may bring a quick retort
As I watch the people passing by

Their bodies move so quickly by
Moving fast, no time, to get caught
Sometimes a laugh, or just a sigh

Rushing round until they die
Forgetting who or what they sought
As I watch the people passing by
Sometimes a laugh or just a sigh

J P Brooks

COME LORD JESUS

Come Lord Jesus, come Thou to me,
Fill us now, with your true love.
Open Thou our eyes, so I can see.

From this evil life, set me free,
Thou alone, came from high above.
Come Lord Jesus, come Thou to me.

In our hearts, we must love Thee,
Thou alone, who art my Holy dove.
Open Thou our eyes, so I can see.

Let me now, your true servant be,
To show the world, all your love.
Come Lord Jesus, come Thou to me.

Come Lord, to live forever in me,
With the ghost, of Thy Holy dove.
Open Thou our eyes, so I can see.

This then Jesus, is my only plea,
To the dear Lord, I give my love.
Come Lord Jesus, come Thou to me.
Open Thou our eyes, so I can see.

F Schofield

As One Millennium Wanes

As one millennium wanes, why should we care?
Another waxes: shall we live to see
Mankind, contrite, our grosser faults repair?

And shall we breathe the unpolluted air
And all unsullied keep the earth and sea?
As one millennium wanes, why should we care?

Not for ourselves the burden do we bear:
For those unborn, on whose behalf may we,
Mankind, contrite, our grosser faults repair.

Let war no longer with red talons tear
And mutilate the future: set us free.
As one millennium wanes, thus should we care.

While time slips by, may we the truth declare;
Confess, alone we cannot find the key
And thus, contrite, our grosser faults repair.

So knock, and be it opened, then, aware,
(Our lesson learnt at last), that only He
As one millennium wanes, supports our care,
That we, with Him, may yet our faults repair.

Kathleen M Hatton

KILLER
(Jean Paisley's Killer Villa)

Give up murder for the millennium,
people could walk the streets at night,
let joy ring through your cerebellum.

Save all those tests done on our cranium,
not just because of a nasty fight,
give up murder for the Millennium.

leave the piranha at the aquarium,
with a fervour burning bright,
let joy ring through your cerebellum.

Slowly like a craft of helium,
we must try to put things right,
give up murder for the Millennium.

Stop the ever-swaying pendulum,
save us from this Godless blight,
let joy ring through your cerebellum.

It will lead you to a requiem when we
give out the potassium,
the bodies are an awful sight,
give up murder for the millennium,
let joy ring through your cerebellum.

Jean Paisley

ATOMIC DESTRUCTION

A wise man voiced the noble thought,
To end the fallen angel's reign;
The deadly deed the dreamer wrought.

Return to God what He has bought
With tender, sacrificial pain:
A wise man voiced the noble thought.

To this end the two men sought
Solution to our Earthly bane:
The deadly deed the dreamer wrought.

On good and bad alike, we're taught,
Beams the sunshine, falls the rain:
A wise man voiced the noble thought.

We have, in human power, caught
Atomic might. God's love sustain
The deadly deed the dreamer wrought.

Let Satan rule - or bring to naught
This Earth and all her glories, vain.
A wise man voiced the noble thought;
The deadly deed the dreamer wrought.

Christine Knight

CAFÉ GONDREÉ PEGASUS BRIDGE

Those airmen doing what is right:
Fell from the sky like silent moths,
And struggled in the misty night.

Across the bridge ghostlike and white:
Acrid smoke reveals the wrath;
Those airmen doing what is right.

That wicked marsh plagued with spite
Caressed each form way up aloft -
And struggled in the misty night.

One burst of flame - then all was quiet
Each heart beating fast and soft -
Those airmen doing what is right.

Pegasus caught and held so might
The river below - now red with froth -
And struggled in the misty night

One last glider dips in flight
The battle won - proud of thy cloth,
Those airmen doing what is right
And struggled in the misty night.

Valerie Cubitt

THE BALANCE OF LIFE

The sun provides our daytime light,
The earth rotates for night and day,
The moon casts beams to us at night.

The sun begets both joy and might
To help us step along our way:
The sun provides our daytime light.

But when the light's no longer bright,
For sleep we on our beds do lay:
The moon casts beams to us at night.

And when the sun is at its height,
It makes us feel so happy and gay:
The sun provides our daytime light.

But when the evening comes in sight
We lay down tools, do as we may:
The moon casts beams to us at night.

Our lives need contrast, black and white,
Rest and action, work and play:
The sun provides our daytime light,
The moon casts beams to us at night.

Joan Cole

CONVOY

An exploding blindness of stinging grey risen from the deep.
Life, a momentary glow of heat, declines and begins to fade.
Cocoon of ice, frozen flesh and steel, waiting death to reap.

Arctic aggression readies for the encounter of oncoming sheep.
Death by nature, a hazardous outcome being entirely manmade.
An exploding blindness of stinging grey risen from the deep.

Sunken remains of the struggle, fallen secrets the water will keep.
Foam no more to cut, buckled bows lay adrift with blunted blade.
Cocoon of ice, frozen flesh and steel, waiting death to reap.

Depth charge fingers clawing plates apart, liquid begins to seep.
Revenge of destroyer crews, hedgehog barrier down and laid.
An exploding blindness of stinging grey risen from the deep.

Airborne parasitic drone delivers an onslaught denying sleep.
Watertight bulkheads entered with ease, torn timbers splayed.
Cocoon of ice, frozen flesh and steel, waiting death to reap.

Who in the Admiralty would have placed life so cheap?
Would they on the treacherous arctic convey route have stayed?
An exploding blindness of stinging grey risen from the deep.
Cocoon of ice, frozen flesh and steel, waiting death to reap.

Charles Green

JOURNEY BACK TO THE HEART

Feeling, at last, the mind growing clearer
Seeing this new day the way that we ought
Thus allowing new truths to draw nearer

Taking time calmly - holding peace dearer
Progression will occur through tranquil thought
Feeling, at last, the mind growing clearer

The millennium starts a new era
Just keep memories which please and support
Thus allowing new truths to draw nearer

'Though the path you tread couldn't be sheerer
Inner contentment is what should be sought
Feeling, at last, the mind growing clearer

Be a pioneer and perseverer
Embrace nature's charms where much can be taught
Thus allowing new truths to draw nearer

Strive to be loving and a reverer
Of all the blessings life's journey has brought
Feeling, at last, the mind growing clearer
Thus allowing new truths to draw nearer

Tina Lipman

A LANDSCAPE PHOTOGRAPH

An artist with his brushes drew
his skills were then conveyed
A picture to construe

He showed the sky in azure blue
the ground was grey in shade
An artist with his brushes drew

His trees stood out so tall and true
like soldiers on parade
A picture to construe

His flowers in many a different hue
were fancifully arrayed
An artist with his brushes drew

This was a rural country view
that this artist made
A picture to construe

The picture finished he bids adieu
his brush aside is laid
An artist with his brushes drew
a picture to construe

Lachlan Taylor

OLD TUNES

There are no old boys left to sing for
Ivor and Vera and the likes of you
After eighty or fifty years or more.

For modern ears a mawkish bore
Old soldiers never die - sez you!
There are no old boys left to sing for.

Novello's home fires are no more
But still keep smiling through
After eighty or fifty years or more.

You whose songs sold by the score
The scene over Dover shone ever blue.
There are no old boys left to sing for.

Pop, rock, rap and soul galore
Swamp seamen troupers and the few
After eighty or fifty years or more.

Historic relics kept in store
Will they yet gain audiences new?
There are no old boys left to sing for
After eighty or fifty years or more.

Leslie Johnson

LOQUACIOUS THAW IS HERE

Loquacious Thaw has come along,
Ice and snow will have to go,
Listen to her song.

Jack Frost has had to say so long,
Skis and sledges seem to know
Loquacious Thaw has come along.

As at the striking of a gong,
Snow is cleared from every bough,
Listen to her song.

None of this will take too long,
Streams and rivers start to flow,
Loquacious Thaw has come along.

Loquacious Thaw can do no wrong,
Little shoots and buds will grow,
Listen to her song.

Loquacious Thaw just swings along,
Hard hearts melt at her 'Hello,'
Loquacious Thaw has come along,
Listen to her song.

Stewart Gordon

LOVE IS ETERNAL

Love is eternal
But not always wise
We are not immortal

Quarrels infernal
But time always flies
Love is eternal

Love is maternal
There in your eyes
We are not immortal

Love is paternal
Sometimes goodbyes
Love is eternal

Love is fraternal
For country it dies
We are not immortal

Love is natural
Heaven in disguise
Love is eternal
We are not immortal

Jean Turner

A ROOM

A room full of emptiness.
Innermost silence,
Stagnant and timeless.

No dirt, no mess
No nonsense
A room full of emptiness.

It's more or less
Past tense.
Stagnant and timeless.

Succumb to stress
And foreign friends.
A room full of emptiness.

Live the press
That life lends.
Stagnant and timeless.

A game of chess
To regain my sense.
A room full of emptiness
Stagnant and timeless.

Kurt A Ringmo

RESTLESS SPIRIT

A restless spirit all alone,
Confused to be in such a space,
Aimlessly searching for a home.

Explores areas quite unknown,
Yearning to settle in a place,
A restless spirit all alone.

Finding the paths that birds have flown,
Moving quickly with undo haste,
Aimlessly searching for a home.

Searching heavens and under stone,
Never ending the constant race,
A restless spirit all alone.

Discovers time, another zone,
Left the body without a trace,
Aimlessly searching for a home.

No longer part of flesh and bone,
Energy lost without a face,
A restless spirit all alone,
Aimlessly searching for a home.

Jan H Hitchcock

MY ASS

My mule has eaten all the grass
The time will come when this he will rue
Until the grass regrows he will fast

He is such a stupidly greedy ass
Unfortunately he will be blue
My mule has eaten all the grass

Into his stable he may be cast
Threatened jokingly with becoming glue
Until the grass regrows he will fast

I know that he will be aghast
Finding out what I can do
My mule has eaten all the grass

As the world goes by their hearts he grasps
His saddened face they view
Until the grass regrows he will fast

His appetite will be extremely vast
Knowing this to be good and true
My mule has eaten all the grass
Until it regrows he will fast

Roger S Foster

MY LADY OF THE MOONFRUIT TREE

My love burst forth it seemed to me
I grew so vast and light
I am the lady of the Moonfruit tree.

A lady of the shadow suspended in eternity
Where light is dark and dim is bright
My love broke forth it seemed to me.

In my land of peace and harmony
Pure love no wrong nor right
I am the lady of the Moonfruit tree.

With sorrow I brought forth humanity
Woman's pain gave man insight
My love burst forth it seemed to me.

My fruits are time the nature of reality
Man's passion for the truth not might
I am the lady of the Moonfruit tree.

Uncrowned I stand amidst the stars to be
As Adam's Eve united left to right.
My love burst forth it seemed to me
I am the lady of the Moonfruit tree.

Jill East

FRICASSEE FEAST

I have invited my friends to dine with me
What delicacy shall I give them to eat?
I shall ask my chef to cook a fricassee.

When he provides a menu for me to see
I hope there will be a selection of meat.
I have invited my friends to dine with me.

My chef's recipe for the meal I'll agree
With forcemeat, mincemeat, sweetmeat will be complete.
I shall ask my chef to cook a fricassee.

The food my chef will cook we'll eat with glee,
And savour and enjoy his culinary feat,
I have invited my friends to dine with me.

We will laugh and enjoy our own company
With excellent food and drink we'll be replete
I shall ask my chef to cook a fricassee.

When we can eat and drink no more we will be
Dancing the night away to a solid beat
I have invited my friends to dine with me
I shall ask my chef to cook a fricassee.

Frank Ede

UNDERSTANDING LOVE

Love is a mystery, hard to understand.
We show it in all different ways.
Ignoring all faults we still find it grand.

Missing your partner when they are not at hand.
Enjoying those together days.
Love is a mystery hard to understand.

Staying together your love to expand.
Regarding someone you are eager to praise.
Ignoring all faults we still find it grand.

That family partnership, leading a happy band.
protecting those close to you, demons to slay.
Love is a mystery hard to understand.

Making your family a protected brand.
Bracing those close to you fighting the fray.
Ignoring all faults we still find it grand.

Love is the eagerness to extend a hand.
Your strength and fortitude will others amaze.
Love is a mystery hard to understand.
Ignoring all faults we still find it grand.

T A Napper

A COTTAGE SMALL

Oh! how I'd love a cottage small,
With rooms that total only four,
A rustic porch and chimneys tall.

Nothing else I can recall
Have I ever wanted more,
Oh! how I'd love a cottage small.

No mansion grand with marble hall,
Just a home with creaking floor,
A rustic porch and chimneys tall.

Trailing flowers on grey stone wall,
While climbing roses skyward soar,
Oh! how I'd love a cottage small.

A roof of thatch above it all,
That cottage with a stable door,
A rustic porch and chimneys tall.

Safe, content, my eyelids fall,
Having finished daily chore,
Oh! how I'd love a cottage small,
A rustic porch and chimneys tall.

Avis Ciceri

CHRISTMAS VILLANELLE

Come celebrate this Christmas time
With angels singing from on high,
For God sent our Saviour divine.

We'll decorate with cones of pine
Then gifts and festive food we'll buy,
Come celebrate this Christmas time.

On Christmas day the bells will chime
For this Child who was born to die,
For God sent our Saviour divine.

Heaven glowed with the wondrous sign,
His natal star hung in the sky,
Come celebrate this Christmas time.

Enjoy a glass of spice mulled wine,
And eat it with a warm mince pie,
For God sent the Saviour divine.

Now come and sing this song of mine,
Shut the good news as folk pass by,
Come celebrate this Christmas time
For God sent our Saviour divine.

Mary Weeks

MY DEAR DEPARTED

How I miss the love of my life
He's gone from me forever
I was his lasting loving wife

We jogged along through toil and strife
To leave him I could never
How I miss the love of my life

We had good times when bad were rife
We worked at life together
I was his lasting loving wife

The loss of him is like a knife
I feel its cutting sever
How I miss the love of my life

How will I face the rest of my life
I'll use my best endeavour
I was his lasting loving wife

No matter now the cutting knife
My love will last forever
How I miss the love of my life
I was his lasting loving wife

Barbara Hampson

GIDDY-UP NEDDY

Again last past the post, giddy-up Neddy.
Now, you are a shadow of your former self.
One time so fit, good enough; and ready.

Now you're a sad old horse, so unsteady,
Unsure of yourself.
Again last past the post, giddy-up Neddy.

Past winner of the Derby; come on Neddy.
You used to be sure of yourself.
One time so fit, good enough; and ready.

Once you carried, champion jockey Flying Eddy.
So proud of yourself.
Again last past the post, giddy-up Neddy.

On your marks horse, ready steady;
Go, falling over your feet, falling over yourself.
One time so fit, good enough and ready.

One day you'll wake up dead, Neddy.
Such a champion horse; now a shade of yourself.
Again last past the post, giddy-up Neddy.
One time so fit, good enough and ready.

B G Clarke

DEAR GOD I SAY

Envelop the heart, with His words and His deeds
For the light of God's peace, to enfold me,
Please make a new start with all creeds.

Can enhance, the lives of man, one needs,
Who will but say, it's God's love, that be,
Envelop the heart, with His words and His deeds.

The ever go onward, for man sometimes pleads,
Our faith in the Maker, that we can, but see,
Please make a new start, with all creeds.

We see in the parables, Your word, that one reads,
To each, and for me, is our earnest, their plea,
Envelop the heart, with His words and His deeds.

Man knows our Saviour, although there are greeds,
Too many are selfish, from your message they flee,
Please make a new start, with all creeds.

You know that our life, is not all it leads
Deception, rejection, which we all, will agree,
Envelop the heart, with His words and His deeds,
Please make a new start, with all creeds.

Hugh Campbell

SHE TURNED ASIDE

I smiled and tried to catch her eye
For love at sight seemed right in May
She turned aside and passed me by

I followed her to explain why
My pride and heart were hurt, and say
I smiled and tried to catch her eye

My passion she could not deny
And recompense me for the way
She turned and passed me by

When side by side, to sanctify
Our vows, she promised to obey
I smiled and tried to catch her eye

Her love was quickly proved a lie
My idol had a heart of clay
She turned aside and passed me by

Now I regret with many a sigh
The dreams I sacrificed the day
I smiled and tried to catch her eye
She turned aside and passed me by.

Cyril Mountjoy

RUSTY WATERS

The untaught harmony of coming spring
O'er the canopies climbing to the sky
Beside rusty waters gushing to bring

With sparrowed birds upon the wing
Abundance of beauty saw and fly
The untaught harmony of coming spring

By moulded walls green ivies cling
To droop their tentacles by and by
Beside rusty waters gushing to bring

Lambs in yon fields frolic and fling
On petalled dreams sweet insects lie
The untaught harmony of coming spring

Where country church bells merrily ring
Responsive warblers they sing and sigh
Beside rusty waters gushing to bring

Reborn insect youth upon the wing
Vain breasted cuckoos sound their cry
The untaught harmony of coming spring
Beside rusty waters gushing to bring

Ann Hathaway

TIME

Tick-tock, tick-tock, it is the clock
Ticking out the time, seconds, minutes, hours
Reminding us of passing time

From early morning, all night long
Ceaselessly it ticks the endless hours away
Tick-tock, tick-tock, it is the clock

The birds migrate in the seasons
To lands across the seas return again
Reminding us of passing time

The lambs in spring, skip, leap, jump
It is a sign springtime is here
Tick-tock, tick-tock, it is the clock

The sun revolves in orbit, sky, stars in galaxy
Sunrise, sunset, the sundial in the garden too
Reminding us of passing time

The oceans' tides do keep momentum.
The waters upon the shores, sands, recede return
Tick-tock, tick-tock, it is the clock
Reminding us of passing time

Sheila Spence

AROMA/ODOUR

This sweet and sensuous aroma of mine,
on this sunny morning in May,
the aroma's scent smells so fine.

Beautifully coloured flowers, in a line,
their different scents blowing around in every way,
this sweet and sensuous aroma of mine.

Sweet smells showing a sign,
a different colour for a different odour every day,
the aroma's scent smells so fine.

Out in the restaurant ready to dine,
the food is out, smelling so fine, there is nothing left to say,
this sweet and sensuous aroma of mine.

Tasty sauces and French wine,
everything is forgotten until you have to pay,
the aroma's scent smells so fine.

Many fragrant perfumes with names like Chanel Nine,
which for the rest of the evening, the fragrance will stay,
this sweet and sensuous aroma of mine,
the aroma's scent smells so fine.

Kimberly Harries

MANX FAIRIES

On Mannin's jewel of the sea
Are little folk, beware!
Fairies there they'll always be.

On Snaefell's Mount and o'er the lea
Fairies fly, everywhere,
On Mannin's jewel of the sea.

On Laxey wheel they play with glee,
They think they're at the fair.
Fairies there they'll always be.

On trams and trains they travel free,
They never pay their fare
On Mannin's jewel of the sea.

At Fairy Bridge they wait to see
If you will greet them there.
Fairies there they'll always be.

At night they hide 'neath trammon tree,
Malign them if you dare!
On Mannin's jewel of the sea
Fairies there they'll always be.

Annie Lund

MY DAD

My dad is away at sea,
'I'll see you' he said, 'won't be long.'
But never does he come home to me.

Mum said he'd gone to set people free,
To help put right an evil wrong,
My dad is away at sea.

We ask, Mum and I, for his safety,
Each Sunday with prayers and song,
But never does he come home to me.

'Mum,' I asked 'how long will Dad be?'
'Son, you must' she said 'be strong.'
My dad is away at sea.

Dad please from your war flee,
Come home to me where you belong,
But never does he come home to me.

As a boy the truth I would not see,
I accept now as the years roll along,
My dad is away at sea,
But never does he come home to me.

Frederick Sowden

MY SWEET GEM

My sweet Gem, goodnight and sleep well
Memories of love and affection do abide
As we walk in memory thro' the dale and dell

So many canine stories in my heart to tell
Of younger days as we played seek and hide
My sweet Gem, goodnight and sleep well

A crisp spring morning, running pell-mell
A bright summer day with a breeze to ride
As we walk in memory thro' the dale and dell

We wander on seashores searching for shells
With you, my gentle Gem dancing by my side
My sweet Gem, goodnight and sleep well

This unconditional love no-one can buy or sell
For ever more you will be my sweet guide
As we walk in memory thro' the dale and dell

Memories linger of that sad death bell
When your breath was no more than a sigh
My sweet Gem, goodnight and sleep well
As we walk in memory thro' the dale and dell

Sylvia Partridge

UNTITLED

Where can I go my fears to face
and inner thoughts dispel?
This world is not a worthy place.

Standing within a timeless space
on a rock twixt heaven and hell
Where can I go my fears to face?

No longer part of the human race
no place on earth to dwell
This world is not a worthy place.

In limbo now, no thoughts to trace
emotions surge and swell.
Where can I go my fears to face?

How sad it is to fall from grace
such loss no man can tell
This world is not a worthy place.

Since I must go to state my case
and leave this fragile shell.
Where can I go my fears to face?
This world is not a worthy place.

Charles MacIntyre

FOR THE YEAR TWO THOUSAND

Two thousand years of words are still ringing
Into patterns of poetry or headlines of hate,
For they are reflecting the lives we are living.

Around the world words are sent spinning
To make wars or a peaceful estate.
Two thousand years of words are still ringing.

Millions and trillions of stories are giving
History, mystery, fantasy, fate,
For they are reflecting the lives we are living.

Tender and loving are words that are singing,
With glorious music to make and create.
Two thousand years of words are still ringing.

Words that are timeless, words that are bringing
Understanding to faith and wisdom's debate,
For they are reflecting the lives we are living.

Now may we see that mankind is beginning
To weave words of peace before it's too late.
Two thousand years of words are still ringing,
For they are reflecting the lives we are living.

Anne Smith

LIFE'S LIFE

Christian life, the way of God
For humans who the world forsook
That life would be the way of God

In losing way in sin we trod
Each bone, each brain in horror shook
Christian life, the way of God

With faith we hold the word of God
All ways whichever road we took
That life would be the way of God

As years pass by, should think of God
Cleanse each sin in babbling brook
Christian life, the way of God

The truth is only seen in God
Human life is like a crook
That life would be the way of God

At close of day give thanks to God
Pray for a love, a love of God
Christian life, the way of God
That life would be the way of God

Geof Farrar

SCARLET BUTTERFLIES

Scarlet butterflies still are here
The last bees - weary - seek their hive.
Whilst winter hovers, close and near.

Sharp sun reflected in the weir
Where humming insects all contrive.
Scarlet butterflies still are here.

Ladybirds hunt amongst leaves sear
Seeking cloned aphids still alive.
Whilst winter hovers, close and near.

Blue shining skies delay their fear
The solstice comes, yet daisies thrive
Scarlet butterflies still are here.

To rocks, small, pale blue flowers adhere
Grey ghosts, the seabirds wheel and dive.
Whilst winter hovers, close and near.

So soon all treasures disappear
And of bright bounty, me deprive
Scarlet butterflies still are here
Whilst winter hovers, close and near.

Jean Rhodes

A New Angel Is In Heaven Now

A new angel is in heaven now
She left this life some time ago
I hope one day she'll return, somehow

With courage she took her final bow
I cried all day, but now I know
A new angel is in heaven now

I miss your voice, if I only knew how
To tell you how my heart hurts so
I hope one day she'll return, somehow

I prayed for mercy, please Lord allow
More time, but all hope was getting low
A new angel is in heaven now

To leave you was my solemn vow
Before it was time for you to go
I hope one day she'll return, somehow

You've gone away, I know that now
The love we shared will never go
A new angel is in heaven now
I hope one day she'll return, somehow

Karen Husband

AUTUMN LEAVES

Fallen leaves lay scattered all around,
Their lives now cast ending's due,
Nature's carpet on the autumn ground.

Winds of change sheer beauty so profound,
Branches with a seasonal view,
Fallen leaves lay scattered all around.

Sycamore wings their flights abound,
Windswept with fate their journeys to,
Nature's carpet on the autumn ground.

Beech nuts amass are readily found,
Squirrels hoard to last winter through,
Fallen leaves lay scattered all around.

Trees stand bare branches ungowned,
Stripped of their glory, beauty too,
Nature's carpet on the autumn ground.

Death has now taken them to mound,
To nourish the earth help life anew,
Fallen leaves lay scattered all around,
Nature's carpet on the autumn ground.

Kenneth Burditt

HE LEFT UPON A SUMMER'S DAY

He left upon a summer's day.
He broke my heart in two,
The hour he went away.

He broke your heart in two you say?
He also broke mine too.
He left upon a summer's day.

I close my eyes and then I pray.
Why was it this he had to do?
The hour he went away.

You seem in such a disarray
Yet still I know it's true,
He left upon a summer's day.

Now there is nothing I can say.
My heart went with him too
The hour he went away.

Oh cruel life, the games you play
For you already knew.
He left upon a summer's day,
The hour he went away.

Elizabeth Hughes

FLEETING YOUTH

Old age slowly come, our plea
        Youth fleeting unable retain
To grow old more gracefully.

Friends near, priority
        Tasks more difficult, in vain
Old age slowly come, our plea.

Lost love, memories not to flee
        Ease tears, grief loneliness pain
To grow old more gracefully.

Lasting love, its constancy
        Ever be, sharing worry blame
Old age slowly come, our plea.

Loving, caring always feel
        Fidelity long remain
To grow old more gracefully.

Freedom from illness, wrath greed
        Wooing life's sweet success fame
Old age slowly come, our plea
        To grow old more gracefully.

Ivy Lott

A FATHER'S LAMENT
IN IRELAND THREE BROTHERS DIE

That fireball of greed,
that in an ecstasy of pain, my children ran.
It devoured up my seed,

now I pray with all my need,
that God to me would show His mighty plan.
That fireball of greed,

that now begs my soul to plead,
illuminates the ferocity of man.
It devoured up my seed,

from this world my sons were freed.
Now in Hell my torments ever hang.
That fireball of greed;

was it the Devil's deed?
Did this curse, drip from his evil fang?
It devoured up my seed,

now with vengeance my heart doth bleed.
I rage at every song of peace that's sung.
That fireball of greed . . .
it devoured up my seed.

Bryon J Jones

COMPLETE IN JESUS

Come to the Mercy Seat
Nothing to fear
Make life complete.

Sit at His feet
Saviour so dear.
Come to the Mercy Seat.

Does His great feat
Cause you to cheer?
Make life complete.

Are you replete?
And Jesus hear?
Come to the Mercy Seat.

Do Jesus meet
For He won't sneer.
Make life complete.

Receive His heat
Transgressions clear.
Come to the Mercy Seat
Make life complete.

Yvonne O'Brien

WHAT WAS

What was never forgotten:
Rest with tender ease,
Upon sheets of cotton.

Face to face emotions unknot,
Indulged with partner to please:
What was never forgotten.

Awake like newborn in spacious cot,
Sleep fulfilled both deeply feel,
Upon sheets of cotton.

Daily separation occurs a lot;
Though togetherness shows for all to see:
What was never forgotten.

Arrive home working day unfrocked,
Gentle kiss follows love left to reseal;
Upon sheets of cotton.

Like handless clock,
To lose one another seems unreal:
What was never forgotten,
Upon sheets of cotton.

Alan Jones

SHED NOT A TEAR

Must not show my fear
As Mum's tumour grows
I'll shed not a tear

Tests, X-rays, unclear
I will not let her know
Must not show my fear

I shall be strong, persevere
My love for Mum will overflow
I'll shed not a tear

I wish to be sincere
Inside my heart bleeds so
Must not show my fear

Stench of death creeps near
Her face white as driven snow
I'll shed not a tear

Together always Mum we are
In life and death I'll follow
Must not show my fear
I'll shed not a tear.

Sonia Coneye

TIME-DRIFT

Accept that waters flow and minutes fly,
Retrieve the messages of passing time
And wonder at the petals drifting by.

Remember flower-bursts where dead armies lie,
How poets shouting from the blood and slime
Accept that waters flow and minutes fly;

Musicians wonder back or reason why
New microtones and pulses blend and chime
And wonder at the petals drifting by.

Children who shrill in games or search and pry
And in discovery grow towards their prime
Accept that waters flow and minutes fly;

Across the years flame passing, lovers try
To tend the seeds that bloom, the plants that climb
And wonder at the petals drifting by.

Prophets have visions, of dreams beyond the sky
And, hearing star-shine sing and planets rhyme
Accept that waters flow and minutes fly
And wonder at the petals drifting by.

John H Hope

HAPPY TIMES

Oh, happy times are here to stay
The peace of green glades I can see
I like to think so anyway

Birth of spring brings the sunny day
The flower lures the bumble bee
Oh, happy times are here to stay

The skies are ostracised of grey
While butterflies fly young and free
I like to think so anyway

Both large and small, birds wing their way
Feeding fledglings across the lea
Oh, happy times are here to stay

The vole and mouse who like to play
Cheat the owl as they swiftly flee
I like to think so anyway

Winter's dead - an end of dismay
An answer to my winter plea
Oh, happy times are here to stay
I like to think so anyway

William Sheffield

THE PEN IS MIGHTIER THAN THE SWORD

The pen is mightier than the sword,
Philosophers tell us so,
Still the pain must be endured.

When every pathway has been explored,
Though the battle be won or no,
The pen is mightier than the sword.

If your motives have been deplored,
Though your heart be true,
Still the pain must be endured.

There is no need to cry upon the floor,
Though your heart be cold and blue,
The pen is mightier than the sword.

When the right and wrong of it is obscured,
Surely your righteousness will shine through,
Still the pain must be endured.

So fight the good fight for the Lord,
Your word will still get through,
The pen is mightier than the sword,
Still the pain must be endured.

Bill Hayles

THE LADY BY THE LAKE

I saw her standing by the lake,
Her golden locks moved in the breeze,
I felt her beauty my breath take.

I feared from dreaming I'd awake,
Above her swayed the willow trees:
I saw her standing by the lake.

'If I lose you my heart will break,
I'll get down on my bended knees,'
I felt her beauty my breath take.

'For you all others I'll forsake,
Oh! Take my hand, I beg you please:'
I saw her standing by the lake.

'A nest for both of us I'll make,
My arms, my heart, I offer these,'
I felt her beauty my breath take.

'Your skin is like the first snowflake,
In winter when the lake doth freeze:'
I saw her standing by the lake,
I felt her beauty my breath take.

John Napier Williams

HOW OFTEN

How often see our grateful eyes
What heaven's light for us has done;
How often does God's love surprise.

Shining rays on life's enterprise
From dawn of day to set of sun;
How often see our grateful eyes.

How often gracious rains baptize
An inward radiance begun;
How often does God's love surprise.

As Grace, Truth, Power evangelize,
From weariness the battle's won;
How often see our grateful eyes.

Heaven's op'ning to our heart supplies
a father's nearness to his son;
How often does God's love surprise.

Compassion shines down from the skies,
A greater mercy there is none.
How often see our grateful eyes;
How often does God's love surprise.

Ken Millar

FRIENDSHIP

I had a birthday recently.
Amongst good wishes I received,
A poem my friend composed for me.

The postman brought more mail - 'twas he;
Now arranged so friends who call will know,
I had a birthday recently.

Lined up on my piano - see!
Verses there galore;
A poem my friend composed for me.

With poetic licence flattery,
The A4 sheet is not up there;
I had a birthday recently.

Folded in my Bible for me to see,
These treasured words I keep there;
I had a birthday recently,
A poem my friend composed for me.

Ivy Squires

FAMILY TIES

O, how I long to be free!
In a world usurping nature's crown
of maternal anxiety

And I would assuage paternity,
though not for me, ambition's clown.
O, how I long to be free!

I seek good company
to lift the heart, ease the frown
of maternal anxiety.

A gay inspiration fills me
(or in paternal conflict, surely drown);
O, how I long to be free!

Father, will you walk with me?
Our jealousy put down,
of maternal anxiety . . .

What matter, the stains of history
on a cherished christening gown?
O, how I long to be free
of maternal anxiety!

R N Taber

Sand, Sea And Life

'Tis deserted now, the golden sand
Bathed in sunset's glow.
For evening falls, and quietness fills the land.

Children's castles on every hand
Await the timeless flow.
'Tis deserted now, the golden sand.

Young ones do not understand,
Or the tide's destruction to know.
For evening falls, and quietness fills the land.

Tomorrow, rising castles grand
Will again, fill the beach below
'Tis deserted now, the golden sand.

Seagulls call above the strand,
Hauntingly fading, and slow.
For evening falls, and quietness fills the land.

Tides roll in at nature's command,
Implacable as a foe.
'Tis deserted now the golden sand,
For evening falls, and quietness fills the land.

Violet Smith

LISTEN WITH YOUR EYES

Don't despair I hear your cries,
When you look to me for aid,
Just listen with your eyes.

You have your lows, you have your highs,
Sounds, that always fade,
Don't despair I hear your cries.

I understand when I hear your sighs,
At life's own big charade,
Just listen with your eyes.

You wonder where your future lies,
Hopes! They seem to fade,
Don't despair I hear your cries.

In your mind you memorize,
Sounds from voices made,
Just listen with your eyes.

When all seems lost, under grey quiet skies,
You have dropped on knees and prayed,
Don't despair I hear your cries,
Just listen with your eyes.

William Lea

ETERNITY'S LIE?

Beyond this earth, the enveloping sky,
An immensity of cosmic space,
With the eternal query, why? Why? Why?

Let my spirit soar and soul to fly
Above this very special place,
Beyond this earth, the enveloping sky.

As time flows agonizingly by,
With multiplying doubts to face,
With the eternal query, why? Why? Why?

Who can believe, and logic defy,
That mortals can join, and the heavens embrace?
Beyond this earth, the enveloping sky.

Will the fates in time deny
Man's sacred destiny, and final grace,
With the eternal query, why? Why? Why?

Perchance we'll unfold a cruel lie,
When humanity's run its final race,
Beyond this earth, the enveloping sky,
With the eternal query why? Why? Why?

Iolo Lewis

SOLITAIRE

I eat my breakfast alone
Trying to bear the pain
Perhaps one day you will phone

Without you I am forlorn
Nothing tastes the same
I eat my breakfast alone

I miss you now you have gone
I am the one to blame
Perhaps one day you will phone

Now I am on my own
Every day seems just the same
I eat my breakfast alone

I wish you would come back home
Together we have much to gain
Perhaps one day you will phone

Why did you have to roam?
Our love is like a flame
I eat my breakfast alone
Perhaps one day you will phone

Kate McDonnell

MEMORIES OF MY DEAR WIFE

I watched you fade away and die.
There was nothing I could do.
I just thought of happy times gone by.

The cancer took you, I don't know why.
For you were gentle, kind and true.
I watched you fade away and die.

I watched your courage with a sigh.
As all life's strength ebbed from you.
I just thought of happy times gone by.

A heart of gold gave one last sigh.
God took your hand and led you through.
I watched you fade away and die.

When you were gone it made me cry.
As each day passed the emptiness grew.
I just thought of happy times gone by.

I'm still sad and often cry.
When winter nights do start anew.
I watched you fade away and die.
I just thought of happy times gone by.

Keith Wilson

BUG STAY AWAY

Millennium Bug, please, stay away from me,
Because I won't know what to do,
You I do not want to see.

Will you play havoc with my telly,
So that my programmes I can't view?
Millennium Bug, please, stay away from me.

What about my kettle, when I fill it to make tea.
Will it go bang, and blow up, because of you?
You I do not want to see.

Then there is the cooker, the video, and my PC,
Will you ram them, jam them? I hope that won't be true.
Millennium Bug, please, stay away from me.

Will the clocks around the house, go wrong suddenly?
Go backwards, stop, or go so fast that time will go askew?
You I do not want to see.

The old century will fade away, the new year in I'll see,
But I will not let you make me blue.
Millennium Bug, please, stay away from me,
You I do not want to see.

Maud Eleanor Hobbs

MY LOVE

My love has pledged her life to me,
To her I pledge my life as well,
My love she will forever be.

> She knows just how to ring my bell,
> She always rings it, oh so well,
> My love has pledged her life to me.

Without her love to keep me well,
My life would be a lonely hell,
My love she will forever be.

> I'm writing her this villanelle,
> To show a love that's hard to tell,
> My love has pledged her life to me.

When she comes out of her shell,
Her loving makes me feel so swell,
My love she will forever be.

> No-one is as sweet as she,
> I hope with her I'll ever dwell,
> My love has pledged her life to me,
> My love she will forever be.

Mick Nash

LONG AGO LOVE

He lives so very far away
In land across the sea
Perhaps I'll go some day.

With us he felt he could not stay
At home he wished to be
He lives so very far away.

Long distance thoughts together play
In fond telepathy
Perhaps I'll go some day.

Our youth we spent in merry May
And life it seemed so free
He lives so very far away.

His picture shows that hair is grey
He treasures one of me
Perhaps I'll go some day

And when at night to God I pray
He features in my plea
He lives so very far away
Perhaps I'll go some day.

Marion P Webb

WHISPERS THROUGH THE NIGHT

Through the whispers of the night
As, a nightingale sings her lullaby
She flaps her wings, and takes flight

Sweet phrases are heard at twilight
When her valide rich notes, echo high
Through the whispers of the night

Across her throat, shows beams of white
Her bill pointed when she flies by
She flaps her wings, and takes flight.

Beauty is seen, under the moonlight
As the moon moves, around the sky
Through the whispers of the night

An owl peeps down, from the height
And stares, with her deep, dark, eye
She flaps her wings, and takes flight

Her soft wings spread, to her delight
As she watches the nightingale fly
Through the whispers of the night
She flaps her wings, and takes flight.

Jean McGovern

TO A SLEEPING CHILD

While you were asleep last night,
I imagined your innocent dream,
In moonbeam-softened bedroom light.

Mischievous fairy laughing sprite,
Danced with courteous esteem,
While you were asleep last night.

My mind took wing in magic flight,
I felt a joyous wonder gleam,
In moonbeam-softened bedroom light.

I flew with elves in pure delight,
An angel played a magic theme,
While you were asleep last night.

No furrow did your dear brow blight,
Nor sorrow cause a tiny seam,
In moonbeam-softened bedroom light.

I dreamed your future heaven bright,
Dear God! I loved you little Liam;
While you were asleep last night,
In moonbeam-softened bedroom light.

Stephen Wright

ON THE LINE

What a sight to see the washing
All clean and bright
On the line and in the wind dashing.

The shirts their arms are waving
To the sheets in flight
What a sight to see the washing.

There are cottons and woollens flashing
Their colours around with might
On the line and in the wind dashing.

The wind gives them wing
They rise to a height
What a sight to see the washing.

The pegs defy the wind's fling
Pinch the clothes with all their might
On the line and in the wind dashing.

Now there is everything
Dry as dry and white so white
What a sight to see the washing
On the line and in the wind dashing.

Joan McLoughlin

DEAR LITTLE HANDS

Dear little hands, tiny feet,
Blissfully he sleeps unaware,
He has made our lives complete.

Often my prayer I did repeat,
Lord gift a child for us to care,
Dear little hands, tiny feet.

Upon his face a smile so sweet,
As I stroke his golden hair,
He has made our lives complete.

I almost did admit defeat,
At times sank into deep despair
Dear little hands, tiny feet.

When at last my little one we meet,
No other love can compare,
He has made our lives complete.

Our love for him cannot surfeit,
In manhood he sees to our welfare,
Dear little hands, tiny feet,
He has made our lives complete.

Barbara Sowden

DEATH OF A YOUNG GIRL

She rests behind the lichen wall.
Beneath a mound of ochre clay.
For her I give my soul, my all.

How sad the owl's eternal call
above my love in earth's decay.
She rests behind the lichen wall.

I did not heed her silent call.
She did not hint, she did not say.
For her, I give my soul, my all.

There wasn't anyone at all,
why did she think that I would stray?
She rests behind the lichen wall.

I cannot drink such acid gall.
Hold fast dear Lord, don't let her stray.
For her I give my soul, my all.

Oh how she lies, so cold so small.
Make room my love, I come your way.
She rests behind the lichen wall,
to her I give my soul, my all.

Margaret Walker

I THOUGHT I KNEW IT ALL

I thought I knew it all,
I'd just left my youth,
I was having quite a ball.

I hated thinking small;
There was nothing I couldn't do.
I thought I knew it all.

I felt like ten feet tall
My mind adored me too.
I was having quite a ball.

The people built a wall
Of hatred that shone through.
I thought I knew it all.

Suddenly I seemed small,
And those people knew
I had no doubt at all.

My ego saw me fall
And that I know is true.
I thought I knew it all
But really I knew nothing.

Raymond Kirby

In Passing

He thought that he could win the day
With flowers bought to heal the rift.
Almost an afterthought. A way.

Preserving habit's interplay
Through token buying, 'say it with'.
He thought that he could win the day.

Through all the usual toils they say
That naturally the fancies shift.
Almost an afterthought. A way

Of saying, come what may,
Every minute cloud can lift.
He thought that he could win the day.

She thought to keep her fears at bay
She'd buy herself a little gift.
Almost an afterthought. A way

Of soothing pain, her frights allay,
Her troubled feelings, make them shift.
He thought that he could win the day.
Almost an afterthought. A way.

Diane Burrow

MAY PEACE FIND A HOME IN YOUR SOUL

May peace find a home in your soul:
Show great expectation the door.
Simplicity shall make you whole.

Tremble when you hear greed's bell toll:
Offer what you can to the poor.
May peace find a home in your soul.

Don't sail seas of silver and gold:
In harbours of wealth greed will moor.
Simplicity shall make you whole.

When love for money takes control;
Desire's a respectable whore.
May peace find a home in your soul.

Make one with creation your goal;
Enjoy what you have don't crave more.
Simplicity shall make you whole.

Give back to nature what you stole;
Seek for the joy you had before.
May peace find a home in your soul.
Simplicity shall make you whole.

Pauline Ilsley

MY FAITH

Each day, my faith is in the Lord
With fresh love all anew.
As strong and mighty like a sword.

I'll be a pilgrim and go abroad
His work I will pursue.
Each day my faith is in the Lord.

Of Bible stores, I'm never bored
My religion is good and true.
As strong and mighty like a sword.

My place in Heaven will be assured
There is a place for you.
Each day, my faith is in the Lord.

I do my best, sometimes ignored,
But God will see me through.
As strong and mighty like a sword.

The year 2000 will not be flawed
You see, I'm never blue.
Each day, my faith is in the Lord
As strong and mighty like a sword.

Freda Bill

TIME FOR JESUS

To be wise is to be true
Seeking guidance from above
In everything you say and do.

Just let God get close to you
Descending on you like a dove
To be wise is to be true.

When friends appear to be too few
Jesus gives you all His love
He'll be there to comfort you.

In solitude God's there for you
Give Him your hand - He's like a glove
To be wise is to be true.

Taking time to be with you
Contemplating Jesus' love
In everything you say or do.

Silence is God's avenue
Soft and gentle from above
To be wise is to be true
Think on these things, please can you?

Hannah Green

ALONG THE WAY

I look for you along the way:
My way is hard to see
If only you were here to show me!

I lost you for a moment,
In that winding path they call life:
I look for you along the way.

Why did you leave me,
Just show me the way to find you,
If only you were here to show me!

You told me that you loved me;
Please guide me on my way:
I look for you along the way.

If by chance you should see her,
Tell her where I am;
If only you were here to show me!

Tell her to hurry, don't delay,
My time is short, and gets shorter each day:
I look for you along the way,
If only you were here to show me!

William Livingston

THE BEST IS YET TO BE

The time has passed too soon for me,
Three score years and twenty more.
The best is yet to be.

Childhood, a bitter memory,
The twenties much disturbed by war.
The time has passed too soon for me.

A loving husband, happy family,
A home with an ever open door.
The best is yet to be.

A daughter far across the seas,
A loved ones smile around no more,
The time has passed too soon for me.

What shall I do now days are free?
No ties to bind me as before.
The best is yet to be.

I'll tell the good news to all I meet,
That in Jesus our future is secure.
The time has passed too soon for me,
The best is yet to be.

Joy Tilley

THE RISING THAT NEVER WAS

I miss the rising of this sun
caught in this monotonous act
as my heart is fused in this clone.

I want to be wrapped in your momentum
and find in it my most prized track
I miss the rising of this sun.

The friendship has just begun
and yet I'm caught in this pact
as my heart is fused in this clone.

Has your soul from me sworn
I never intended it to read this tract
I miss the rising of this sun.

Why does life cease in such endless sums
does not the bird smell the call of tact
as my heart is fused in this clone.

If you heard spring its own tune sung
would not silence speak its lullaby out
I miss the rising of this sun
as my heart is fused in this clone.

Roza Ajibola

THE GRANSHA KILLINGS

Once two young men of sect oppressed in name of crown
drove through the night towards dark destination -
'til by special-forces' bullet-hail mowed down.

Scheduled at a venue not far outside their town,
selected to conduct assassination -
once two young men of sect oppressed in name of crown.

Thought not of fate by which they both were bound -
intent only upon next assignation,
'til by special-forces' bullet-hail mowed down.

No statesmen these, no gesticulating clowns -
just 'soldiers in a war to free a nation' . . .
once two young men of sect oppressed in name of crown.

Not a chance to surrender - no, not a sound
from more than dozen undercover stations,
'til by special-forces' bullet-hail mowed down.

Though youths trained to kill . . . still murdered round by round
by those who had hidden with callous patience!
Once two young men of sect oppressed in name of crown,
'til by special-forces' bullet-hail mowed down!

Perry McDaid

MISSING HER

My love has gone, and set me free
Left me feeling blue
I miss her loving constantly.

Gone to seek her destiny
Don't know what I'll do
My love has gone, and set me free.

Our love is carved upon a tree
For friends of ours to view
I miss her loving constantly.

I wonder if she misses me
And is she pining too
My love has gone, and set me free.

I send to her this heartfelt plea
Forever, please be true
I miss her loving constantly.

Good luck to her, where she may be
I send my best to you
My love has gone and set me free
I miss her loving constantly . . .

Gig

MARTIN AND DEBBIE'S RAINBOW DAY

Our rainbow day will soon be here,
Vivid hues to bind us as one.
Harlequin love, vibrant and near.

After the rain, our sky is clear.
We hold hands, look up at the sun.
Our rainbow day will soon be here.

You've coloured me with your love, dear.
Washed away the black, white and dun.
Harlequin love, vibrant and near.

Warmth surrounds me, I feel no fear,
Ecstatic with the prize I've won.
Our rainbow day will soon be here.

You wiped away my single tear
Before the crying had begun.
Harlequin love, vibrant and near.

Eternal love, year after year;
Gold circle of two souls in one.
Our rainbow day will soon be here.
Harlequin love, vibrant and near.

Debbie Lorns

SOLILOQUY

The anguish of Golgotha is too much for me to bear.
That suffering! For me? How can I ever hope to repay.
Alone my cross I cannot carry, but the Lord is there to share.

The cock crowed three times the night Peter was asked to swear
That he didn't know you and had never walked the way.
The anguish of Golgotha is too much for me to bear.

How to make amends, put right my life, the sinfulness repair.
Is it possible to correct the faults you paid for on that day?
Alone my cross I cannot carry, but the Lord is there to share.

Your love saved him, there was nothing Peter would not dare
No more was he fearful, to the crowds he had his say.
The anguish of Golgotha is too much for me to bear.

To do thy will from day to day with joyfulness and care,
For strength to pay the price of loving you I pray.
Alone my cross I cannot carry, but the Lord is there to share.

Guide my every thought and action as I seek to meet you there.
Forgive me, redeem me and wash my sins away.
The anguish of Golgotha is too much for me to bear.
Alone my cross I cannot carry, but the Lord is there to share.

Jennifer Stella Smeed

A SMILE

A smile will drive away your tear
And turn the welling clouds, I see,
That hides within your darkest fear

The thunder storms, and then it's clear
What are your thoughts that need of me?
A smile will drive away your tear

Some sorrow of a passing year
A price to pay, a price to be
That hides within your darkest fear

Sometimes the road of life is sheer
The door will lock without its key
A smile will drive away your tear

Memories will be always here
But move life on, let troubles flee
That hides within your darkest fear

Just one last kiss, the time is near:
And give me of your smile cherié
A smile will drive away your tear
That hides within your darkest fear.

George Lockwood

POOR CHILDREN OF THE WAR'S LAMENT

(In loving memory of our dear Dad)

Our Dad's away, gone to the war
Mam sits home all day and cries
No smiling faces anymore

To see his face through open door
No longer baking cakes and pies
Our Dad's away, gone to the war

Mam's no money, we're so poor
She tells the rent man loads of lies
No smiling faces anymore

We long for him, she'll pace the floor
While she stifles sobs and sighs
Our Dad's away, gone to the war

No more walks on Daddy's moor
The heathers beaten withers, dries
No smiling faces anymore

Some say he's dead, we're not sure
Does soul survive as spirit dies?
Our Dad's away, gone to the war
No smiling faces anymore

Angela Maria Wilson

FISH IN THE SEA

Broken is our family tree
Love to us has gone
Thoughts pass our minds to other fish in the sea

Where would we find other love in company
Will it gain like an exploding bomb
Or will I always be free

Parents taught us what came from a bird and bee
Looking around for Dick, Harry or Tom
Thoughts pass our minds to other fish in the sea

Grief in my eyes you can only see
There are threads that dangle, a knot over and done
Broken is our family tree

Beauty of heart is taken from me
Dewdrops of tears have won
Thoughts pass our minds to other fish in the sea

Proof of amendments are a consistency
Now that we know where our heart is from
Broken is our family tree
Thoughts pass our minds to other fish in the sea

Heather Edwards

INTENSIVE CARE

'Thank God! He's alive.'
Said the surgeon dressed in green.
'With care, he'll survive.

Number of ribs smashed - five -
Ruptured kidney, destroyed spleen.
Thank God! He's alive!

His legs and feet were rive;
But wired to his support machine;
With care, he'll survive.

Over time, he should thrive.
I'll check his drips at three fifteen.
Thank God! He's alive!

From that bridge, a fearful dive:
How tragic; how unforeseen.
With care, he'll survive.

The Consultant is due to arrive.
Rest now - pull round that screen.
Thank God! He's alive!
With care, he'll survive.'

B Paxman

CHAINED IN STEEL

You never tell *me* how you feel
You know how much *I* love *you*
Your emotions are chained up in steel

No passion from *you* can I steal
You know that *my* heart is true
You never tell *me* how you feel

When I am hurt, *your* words don't heal
You don't seem to know what to do
Your emotions are chained up in steel

Just tell me if your love is real
And if not for *me* then for who?
You never tell *me* how you feel

My ardour is burning with zeal
The day that we met *my* love grew
Your emotions are chained up in steel

When we met *I* could hear a bell peal
Your kiss gave me wings and I flew
You never tell *me* how you feel
Your emotions are chained up in steel

Bonita Hall

UNTITLED

Love I've found - now I feel free.
A state that conquers every thing -
There is no inward fear in me.

It is so clear I now can see
What the gospel can really bring -
Peace I've found - now I feel free.

I know wherever I may be -
The truth has made me want to sing -
There is no inward fear in me.

I now wish everyone could see
That death will have no bitter sting -
Peace I've found - now I feel free.

And so I dance with starry glee.
To constant love I'll always cling -
There is no inward fear in me.

Instead of *I* it is now *We* -
Safe in the shadow of His wing.
Peace I've found - now I feel free -
There is no inward fear in me!

Pat Melbourn

PAST, PRESENT, FUTURE - WHATEVER!

Past, present, future - whatever!
What will be, will be for all,
Yesteryears gone forever.

Time and tide roll swiftly over . . .
We are but dust, to dust will fall,
Past, present, future - whatever!

It must be soon or never
Listen to the call.
Yesteryears gone forever.

When we view His holy mansions
Visions sacred, so mystique,
Past, present, future - whatever!

Must I awake from slumber,
Come out of my retreat
Yesteryears gone forever.

Time now matters not at all,
I bid adieu, until we meet.
Past, present, future - whatever!
Yesteryears gone forever.

Marion de Bruyn

FOR STEVE

Steve is a friend to me
For fate let us meet,
Many things in common do I see.

We share so much, our thoughts and dreams,
And joined by our writing is a treat,
Steve is a friend to me.

Hope is united I guess it seems
Another challenge eagerly we greet,
Many things in common do I see.

Pray, come true our recurring dreams,
For we'll be proud to walk down the streets,
Steve is a friend to me.

Blessed us both with a gift I see,
A pleasure to write, more so a treat,
Many things in common do I see.

Words they just flow, we must agree,
Another day, and again we meet:
Steve is a friend to me,
Many things in common do I see.

Gladys Moody

MY YEARS GO SO QUICKLY AWAY

My years go so quickly away,
I want to hold them or turn back.
I can't give them an order to stay.

And I become older every day,
I see a lot of lines on my neck.
My years go so quickly away.

I feel, I didn't feel yesterday,
My days are flying. It's a bad fact.
I can't give them an order to stay.

My children are older day-by-day.
I try my deep memory to hack.
My years go so quickly away.

I am looking for the hope's ray,
I lose my years. It is a big lack.
I can't give them an order to stay.

I want to hold up in the life's bay,
I want to hide my regret and mask.
My years go so quickly away,
I can't give them an order to stay.

Anna Virkerman

DAWN RAID

Dawn raid, cop chorus, methinks I'm caught,
One should not rob the gent-r-y,
My life's in tatters and my nerves are fraught.

Everything in my house is hot,
My eyes wide open too late to see,
Dawn raid, cop chorus, methinks I'm caught.

Truncheons in hand, they care not a jot,
Just look at my fretting fami-l-y,
My life's in tatters and my nerves are fraught.

A warrant to arrest I think they've sought,
Are there allies none to deliver me?
Dawn raid, cop chorus, methinks I'm caught.

Handcuffed my wrists is this my lot?
'Come you villain you're ordained by decree,'
My life's in tatters and my nerves are fraught.

What have I gained? It is less than nought,
Ten years will pass until I'm free,
Dawn raid, cop chorus, methinks I'm caught,
My life's in tatters and my nerves are fraught.

Patricia A Thompson

CASCADES

Stars in the universe, planetary deep
Shrouded in mystery
The beauty of a waterfall, cascades steep

Phases of the moon, a pulsating bleep
Solar faced sunflower, centre of space
Stars in the universe, planetary deep

River estuary and harbour creeks
Ocean waves, the ebbing tide
The beauty of a waterfall, cascades steep

Oak trees and birch, breezy willows weep
Pretty as a rose, lilies ascend like
Stars in the universe, planetary deep

Mountains high and hillside heaps
Of heather growing wild and free
The beauty of a waterfall, cascades steep

Springtime daffodils awake from their sleep
Green meadows of daisies, yellow and mellow
Stars in the universe, planetary deep
The beauty of a waterfall, cascades steep.

Rebecca Emma Humphrey

FALLEN FROM GRACE

I feel my life has fallen from grace:
Gone are the words that spoke of love,
My eyes will no longer see your face.

Existence around me is just unknown,
Gone is the one that had enough:
I feel my life has fallen from grace.

I sleep at night in hope of dreams,
A shadow of memories linger above:
My eyes will no longer see your face.

Lips once warm had turned so cold,
Since you left, times have been rough;
I feel my life has fallen from grace.

Tears of heartache fall on your picture,
Picking up the pieces can be so tough;
My eyes will no longer see your face.

You blinded me with stunning beauty,
But in the end you gave me the shove:
I feel my life has fallen from grace,
My eyes will no longer see your face.

Robert Sibbald

VILLANELLE

It's instant joy that I see in you
And this lovely joy doth melt my heart
Whenever my darling comes into view

She knows the meaning of love so true
So sure am I we will never part
It's instant joy that I see in you

Shades of rich colours in every hue
Come and blossom into my mind of finest art
Whenever my darling comes into view

My heart beats the faster at the mention of your name Sue
I knew it was you for me from the start
It's instant joy that I see in you

Our hearts beat as one, our minds are at one too
It really is a perfect shot from Cupid's dart
Whenever my darling comes into view

Life now has such a meaning, thee I woo
Oh let's bless our troth with our loving mark
It's instant joy that I see in you
Whenever my darling comes into view

K W K Garner

I Wipe My Eyes In Sorrow
I Hope There Will Be Tomorrow

I wipe my eyes in sorrow
The day is much longer than I thought was possible
I hope there will be tomorrow.

The nights are too long to borrow
My voice answers hoarsely
I wipe my eyes in sorrow.

Am I a bird of harrow?
Like the fragrance of you growing parsley
I hope there will be tomorrow.

The wings you spread are sparrows
Time can only stand still presently
I wipe my eyes in sorrow.

A cough and you're out picking marrow
My life goes on breezily
I hope there will be tomorrow.

Can I help where there is a laurel?
I listen with a voice not listening harshly
I wipe my eyes in sorrow
I hope there will be tomorrow.

David Rosser

A Villanelle In Blossom

Oh give me a sunny spring day,
Breathing life into the cherry tree,
To bring forth the blossom in May.

It lasts a month then goes away,
But what a beautiful sight to see,
Oh give me a sunny spring day.

As daffodils nod and sway,
Their trumpets herald encouragingly
To bring forth the blossom in May.

The rain still falls to my dismay,
Clouds are grey, oh woe is me,
Oh give me a sunny spring day.

Just as winter seems here to stay,
I hear the hum of the honeybee,
To bring forth the blossom in May.

Although short-lived, all I can say,
Its beauty is sheer serenity,
Oh give me a sunny spring day,
To bring forth the blossom in May.

Ian Fyles

WRITER'S BLOCK AGAIN

I have writer's block again,
I did hope I would get it no more,
And not writing causes me pain.

All this concentrating is wrecking my brain,
And my head feels a little sore,
I have writer's block again.

I need to write to stay sane,
The urges to write I can't ignore,
And not writing causes me pain.

As I watch the rainwater run down the window pane,
I feel the urge growing stronger than before,
I have writer's block again.

I don't think the block could be moved by a crane,
It just sits there patiently annoying me more and more,
And not writing causes me pain.

The block just sits there like a stain,
Much more annoying than a birds persistent caw,
I have writer's block again,
And not writing causes me pain.

Melanie Jane Hickling (15)

NEVER BEFORE

I'd never before felt like this,
Then one of us had to spoil it.
Never before known perfect bliss.

Our affair, been sealed with a kiss,
Relationship built bit by bit.
I'd never before felt like this.

Seeing your face, that's what I miss,
Now all I see, bottomless pit.
Never before known perfect bliss.

Looking at your photo I hiss,
Won't forget the sarcastic wit.
I'd never before felt like this.

Thoughts of love I quickly dismiss,
For together we did not fit.
Never before known perfect bliss.

Old friends I had dumped, how remiss,
As a couple we weren't a hit.
I'd never before felt like this,
Never before known perfect bliss.

S Mullinger

A LETTER TO 'B' AND 'D'

I saw your garden yesterday
Lit by the soft autumnal light.
Its beauty took my breath away.

Today I dreamt of that display
Of shrubs and trees of different height.
I saw your garden yesterday.

A rose was blooming on that day
The perfume gave me pure delight.
Its beauty took my breath away.

I wandered on and found my way
To apple trees - I took a bite.
I saw your garden yesterday.

I came upon a fine array
Of blossoms blooming on your site
Its beauty took my breath away.

I thank you for that magic day.
So 'B' and 'D' I had to write -
I saw your garden yesterday;
Its beauty took my breath away.

Evelyn Golding

GOLDEN CALF

The Hebrews danced around a calf of gold:
We in our time have idols of our own -
A business-culture does our world enfold.

Forgetful of God's help, they proved too bold
When pious Moses left them all alone:
The Hebrews danced around a calf of gold.

It's not for us their fickleness to scold:
Our shallowness they might themselves bemoan;
A business-culture does our world enfold.

While God His holy laws to Moses told
In Aaron's heart the seeds of pride were sown:
The Hebrews danced around a calf of gold.

Today a P.R. post this man would hold;
Of businessmen he'd have each one a clone:
A business-culture does our world enfold.

Is it not time at length to break the mould?
Remember how God's Son did once atone.
The Hebrews danced around a calf of gold:
A business-culture does our world enfold.

Anne Sanderson

SECRET LOVE

When first I met you
It was love at first sight,
My heart would forever be true.

But you loved another, who,
Was your heart's delight,
When first I met you.

In my solitude I watched you woo
and wept into the night,
My heart would forever be true.

Perhaps, within myself I knew
Your love would never be my right,
When first I met you.

Then your heart's delight kissed adieu
I comforted you in her flight,
My heart would forever be true.

But alas, I was lost to your view
As a new love you found dazzled bright,
When first I met you
My heart would forever be true.

Jean McDonald

THE SAFE SHEEP

My Lord will gather His sheep in His fold,
Care for them lovingly, keep them in sight.
His mighty arms will secure them and hold.

They'll want for nothing, protected from cold
And from the wolves with their howling at night.
My Lord with gather His sheep in His fold.

They will together, the young and the old,
Feed in green pastures, while it is still light.
His mighty arms will secure them and hold.

His loving care is more precious than gold
To His blessed ones who exist to do right.
My Lord will gather His sheep in His fold.

His strong protection makes His own sheep bold,
Kept by Him safely with all of His might.
His mighty arms will secure them and hold.

Then His own sheep who are made in His mould
Will go to Heaven to live in the height.
My Lord will gather His sheep in His fold.
His mighty arms will secure them and hold.

Joyce M Turner

NO LONELY NIGHTS

Sweet friend of my childhood dreamland,
gold dust sprinkles cast in my eyes
as nights pass with me holding your imaginary hand.

The lonely child held to you with unbreakable band,
no toys here today at my sides
sweet friend of my childhood dreamland.

No days out with parents carefully planned,
no teachers with lessons so wise,
as nights pass with me holding your imaginary hand.

No holidays on beaches with sun-bleached sand,
no arms stretched to help me to rise,
sweet friend of my childhood dreamland.

No tender angel to keep my fevered brow fanned
or loose my tender body from its ties
as nights pass with me holding your imaginary hand.

Rumanian orphanage where nothing is grand
just harried assistants, no mother to advise.
Sweet friend of my childhood dreamland
as nights pass with me holding your imaginary hand.

Channon Cornwallis

VILLANELLE

Where, O where is Heaven's light?
Persistently it hides from me.
This drab life could be so bright.

If only I could catch a sight
Of it to warm my memory.
Where, O where is Heaven's light?

How I long for the delight
Of light to wrap itself round me.
This drab life could be so bright.

The blackness would give way to white
And I'd bathe in a glowing sea.
Where, O where is Heaven's light?

Gone from life would be all fright,
Replaced by joy's philosophy.
This drab life could be so bright.

Dare I hope that Heaven might
Shine its longed-for rays on me!
Where, O where is Heaven's light?
This drab life *could* be so bright.

Maureen Inglis-Taylor

A SPECIAL TIME

The year 2000 will come and go
Folk everywhere their future seeking
Like all the other years so

Folk feeling all aglow
Of doing a special something
The year 2000 will come and go

We all seek to know
Will the year be interesting
Like all the other years so

As the rivers that flow
Folk will go a-wandering
The year 2000 will come and go

Folk rushing to and fro'
Without a moment sparing
Like all the other years so

Some folk will glow
Finding peace everlasting
The year 2000 will come and go
Like all the other years so

Josephine Foreman

MY HEART GOES OUT TO EVERYONE

My heart goes out to everyone,
Wherever they may be,
This troubled world, the setting sun.

And war of hate that has begun,
Will no-one ever see,
My heart goes out to everyone.

The dove of peace has long since gone,
The poor are left to flee,
This troubled world, the setting sun.

Combatants with the loaded gun,
Despair and hatred do I see,
My heart goes out to everyone.

People on the move walk on,
To stateless lands maybe,
This troubled world, the setting sun.

The misery and death do shun,
Bewildered, bitter refugee,
My heart goes out to everyone,
This troubled world, the setting sun.

B Smedley

I CRAVE TO NOISE ELIMINATE

I crave to noise eliminate,
The raucous and offensive kind
That shall not let me meditate

on what is beautiful, ornate
that infiltrates my questing mind;
I crave to noise eliminate.

When there is music magic, great
Why can't we leave discord behind
that shall not let me meditate?

Shall deprivation be my fate,
A listener to disgusting grind?
I crave to noise eliminate.

If only this tumult I hate
was not to enemy confined
that shall not let me meditate.

I can't forgive, exonerate
Such blasphemy so unrefined.
I crave to noise eliminate
That shall not let me meditate.

Ruth Daviat